FASHION
Sketchbook

Savvy Stationery

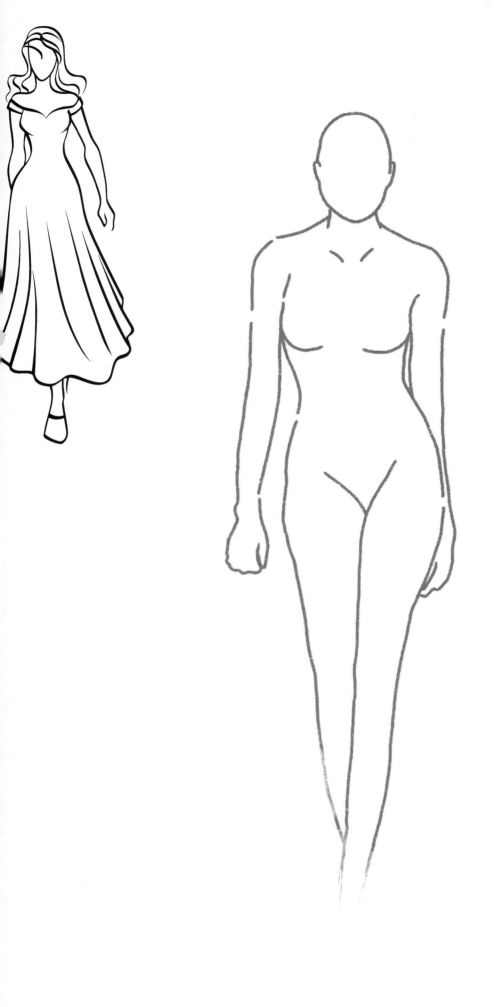

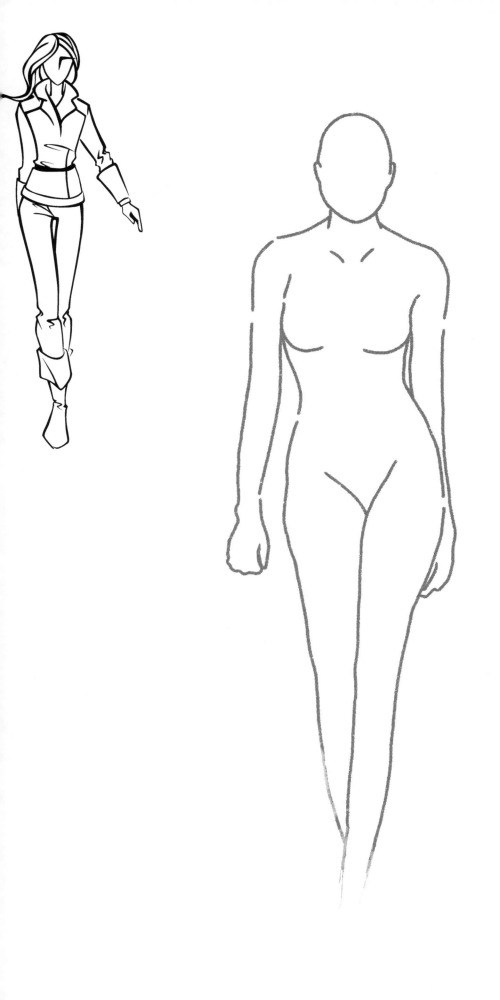

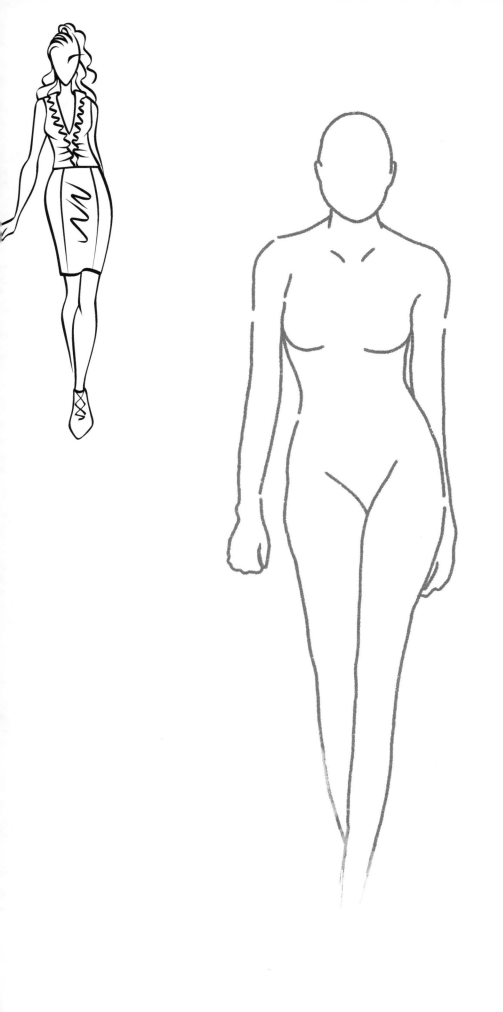

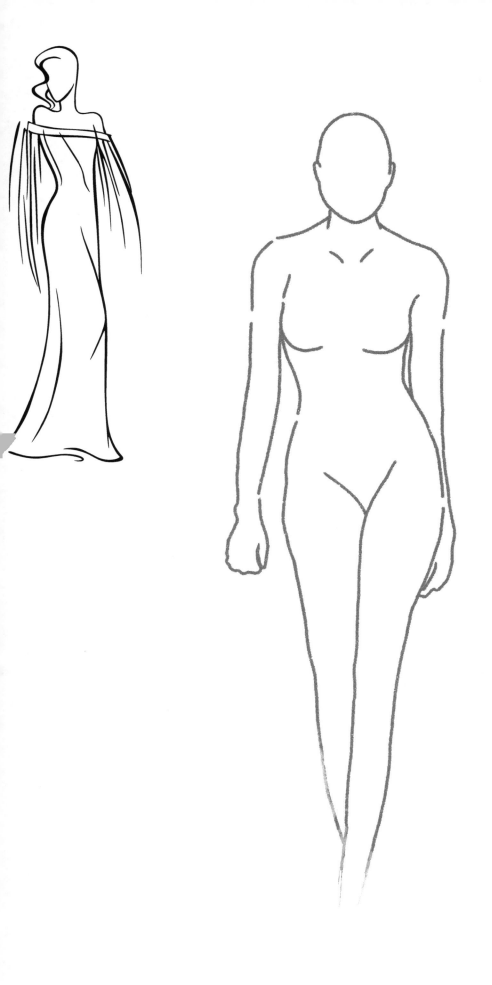

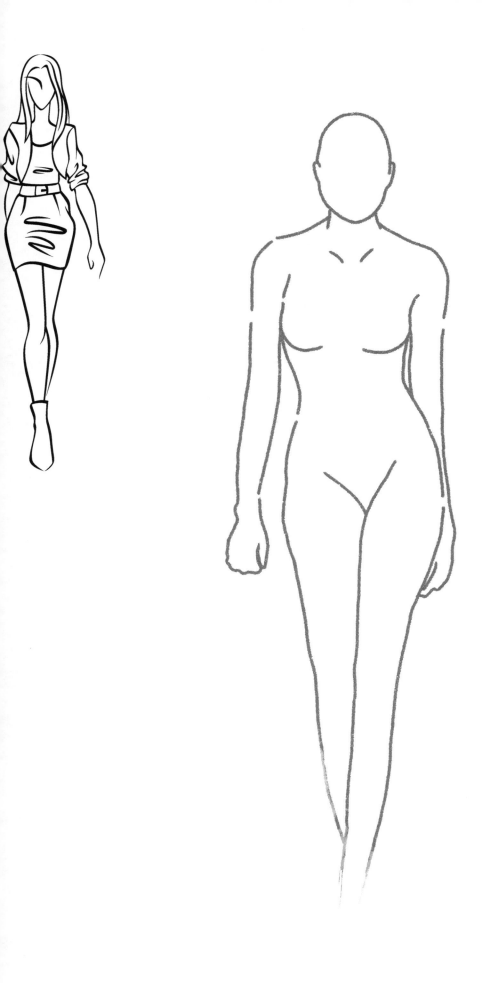

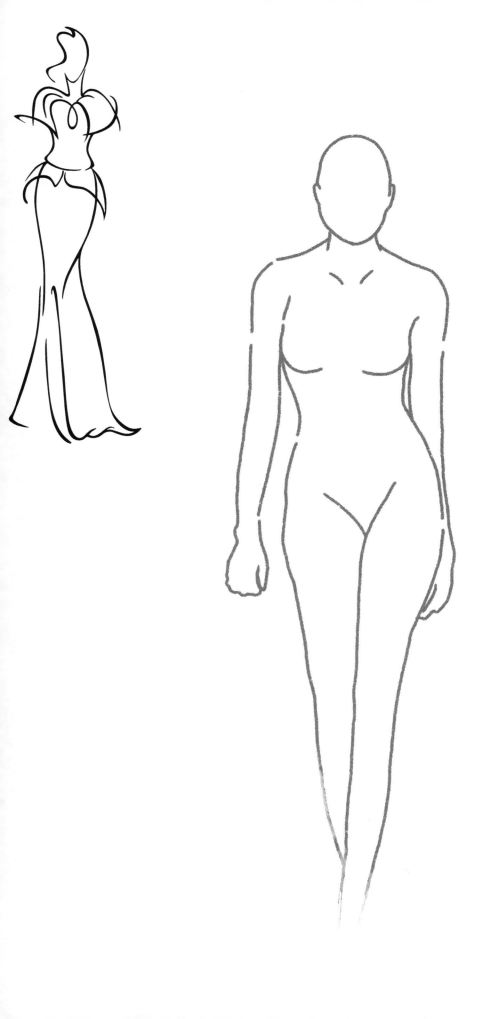

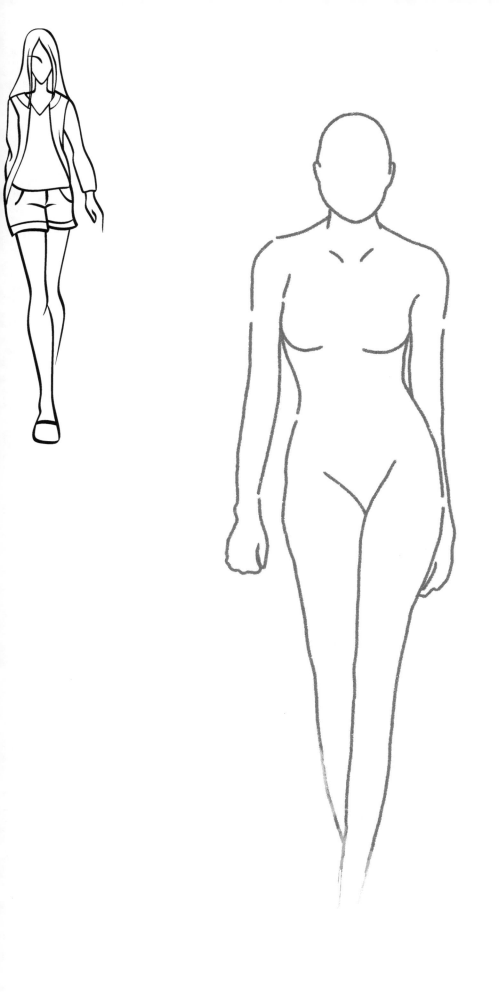

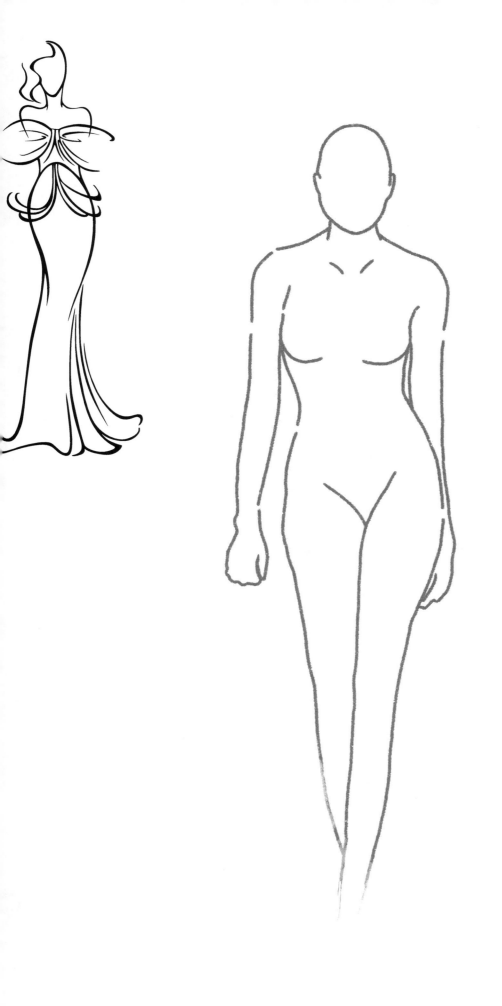

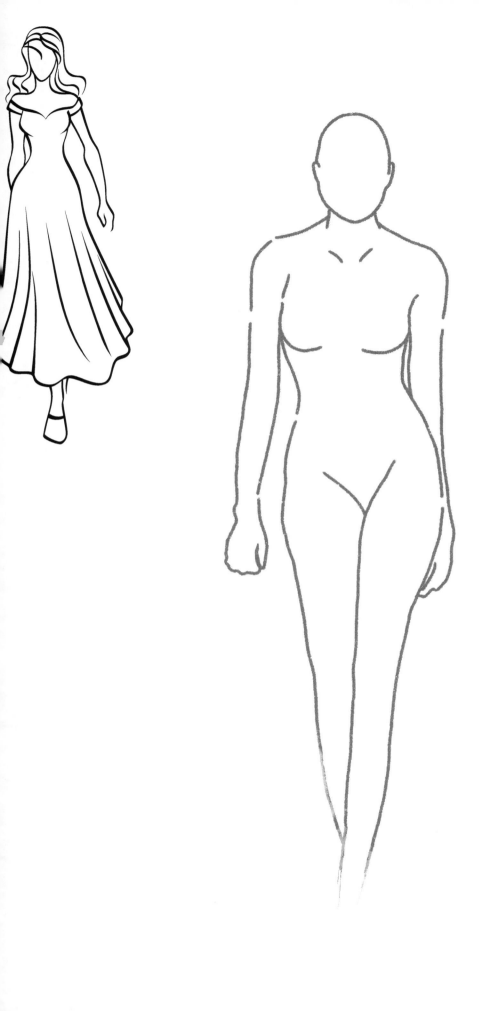

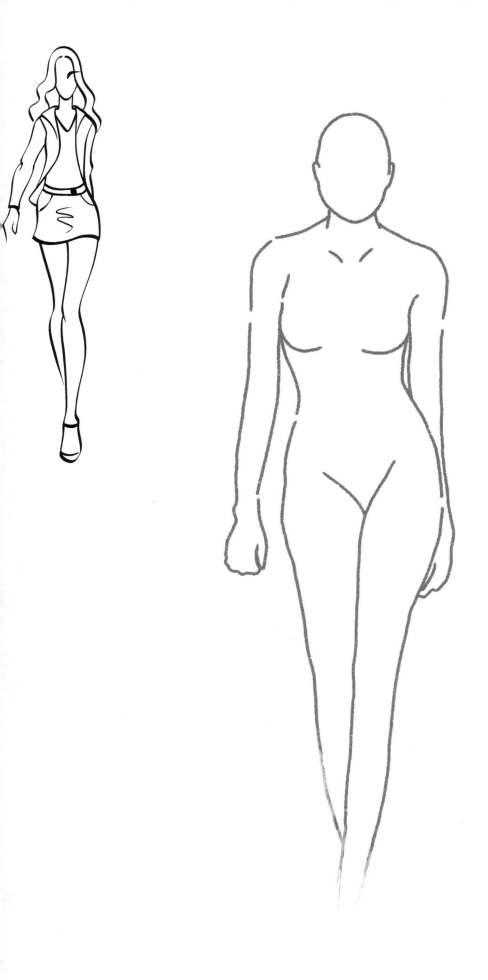

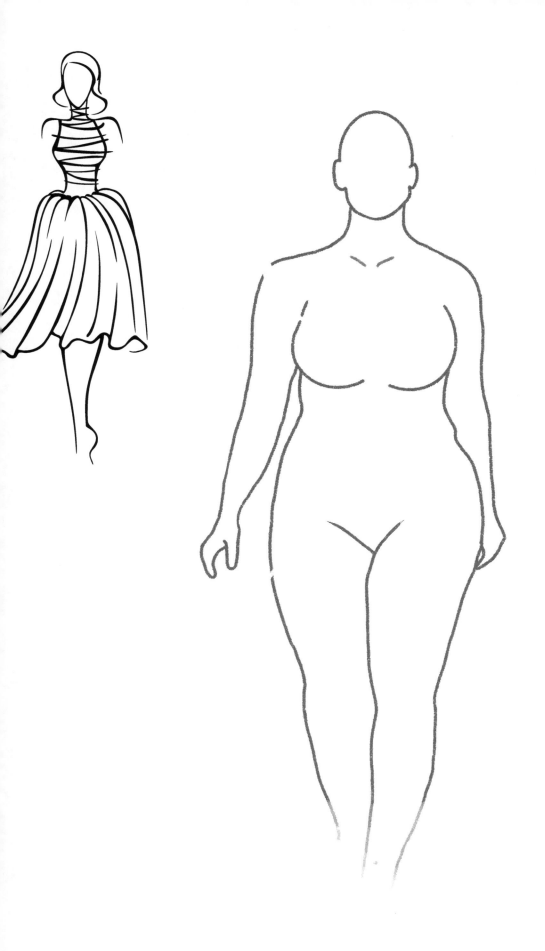

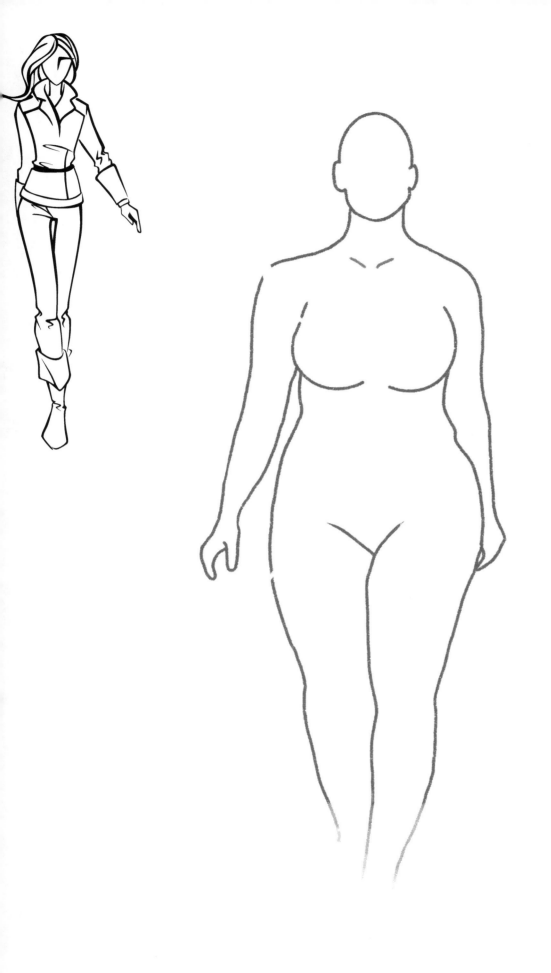

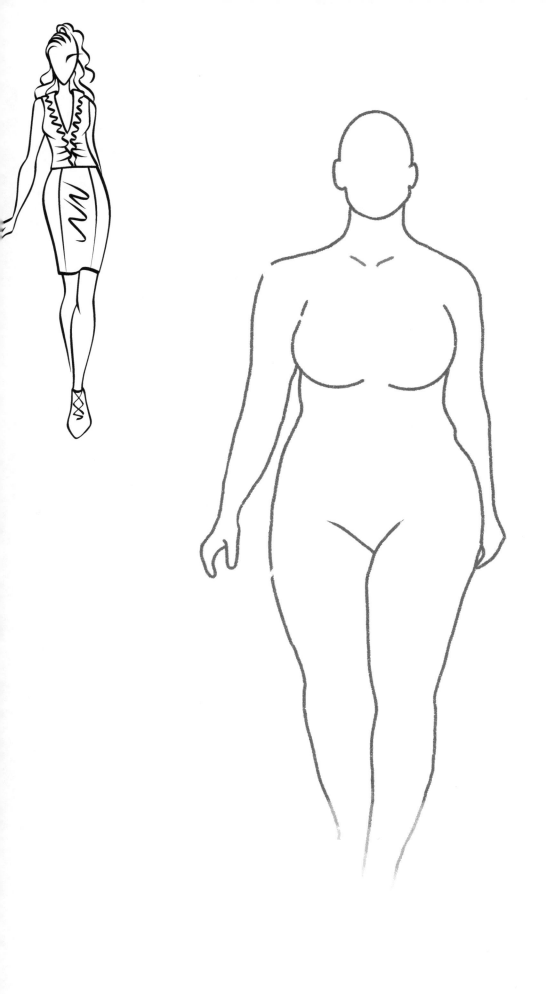

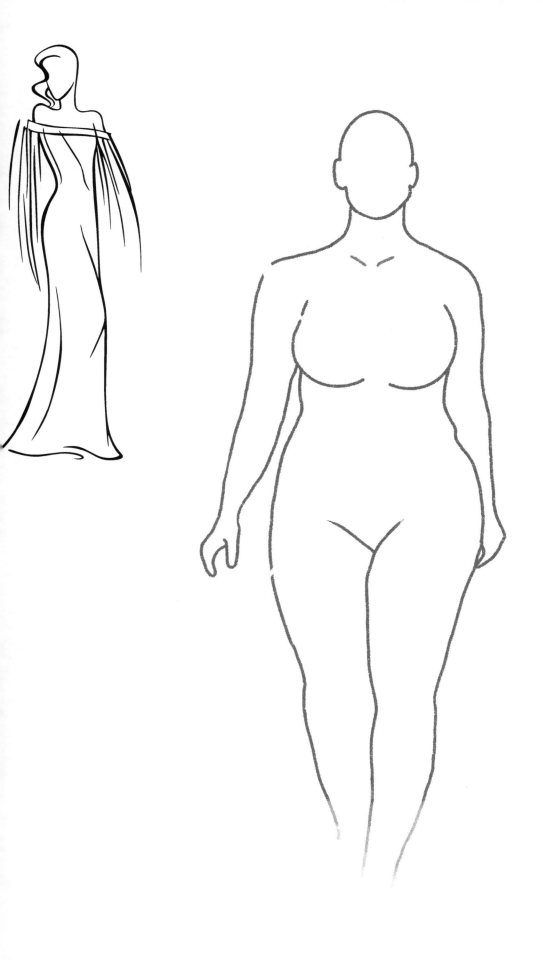

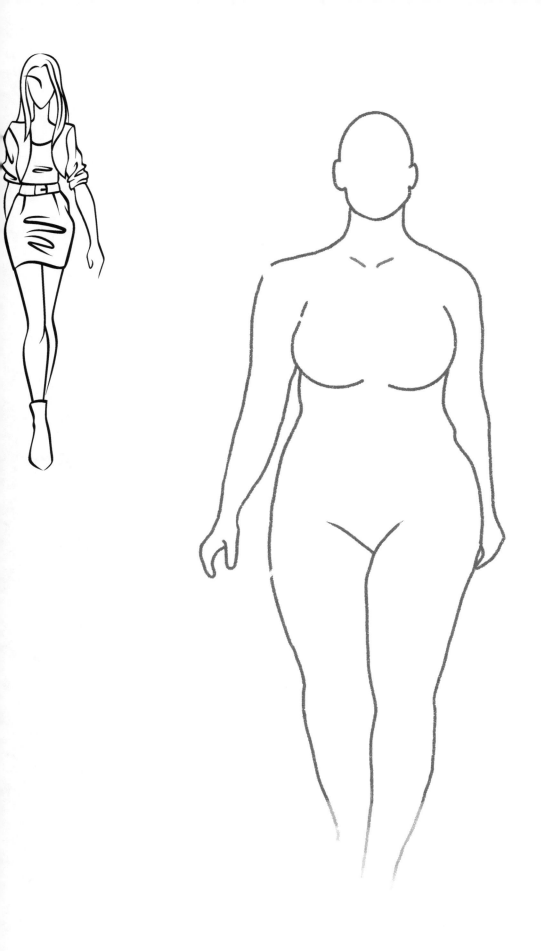

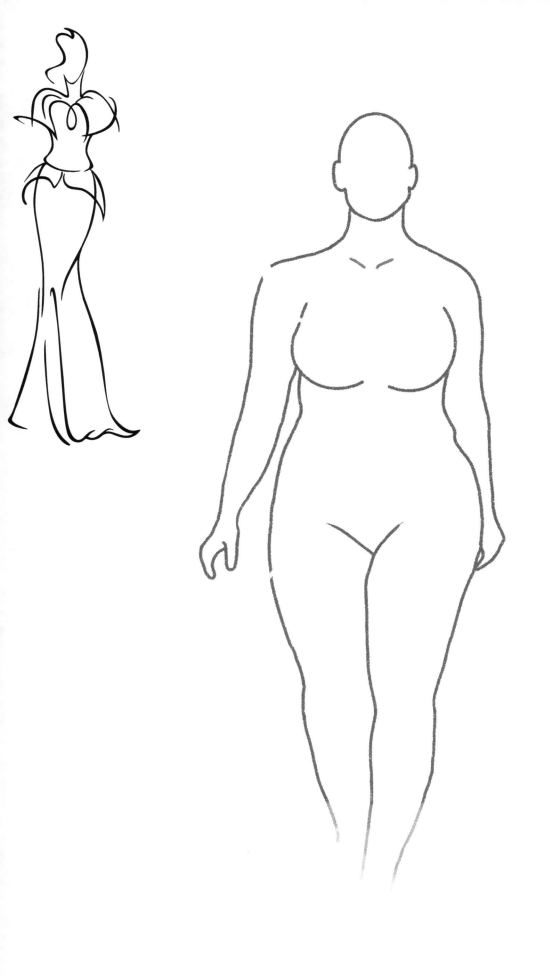

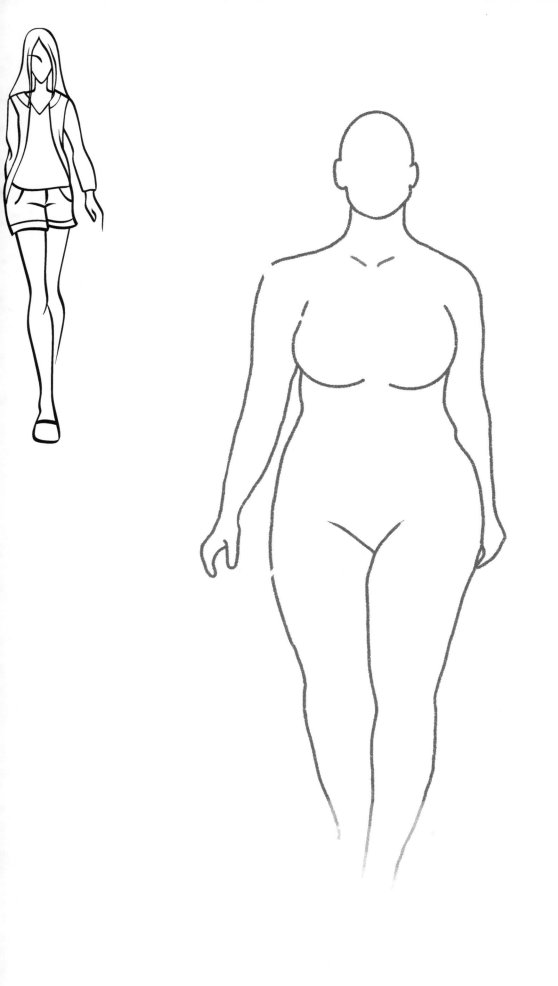

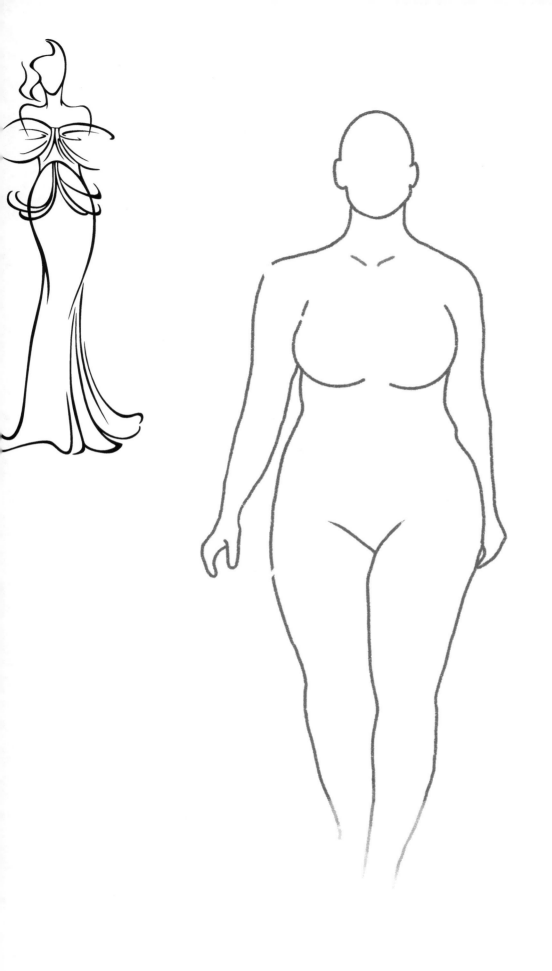

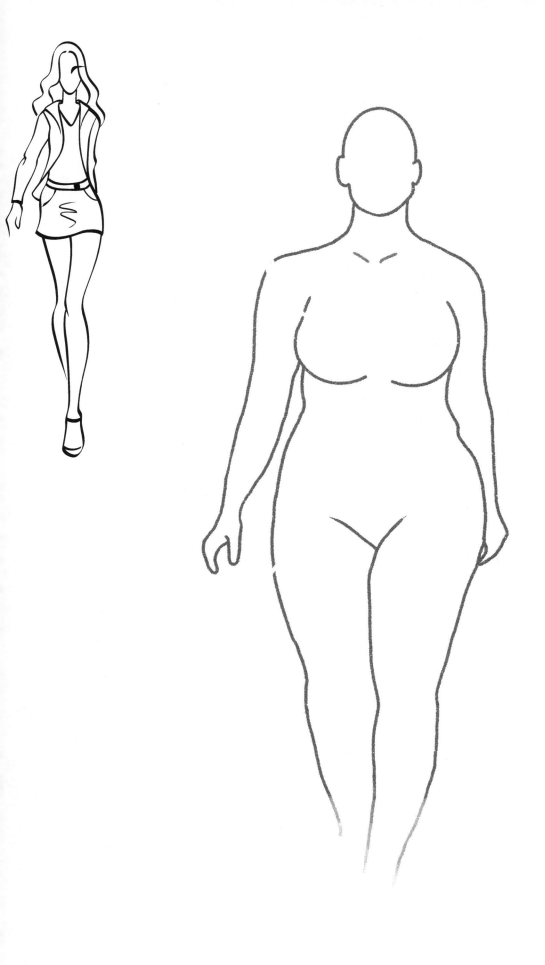

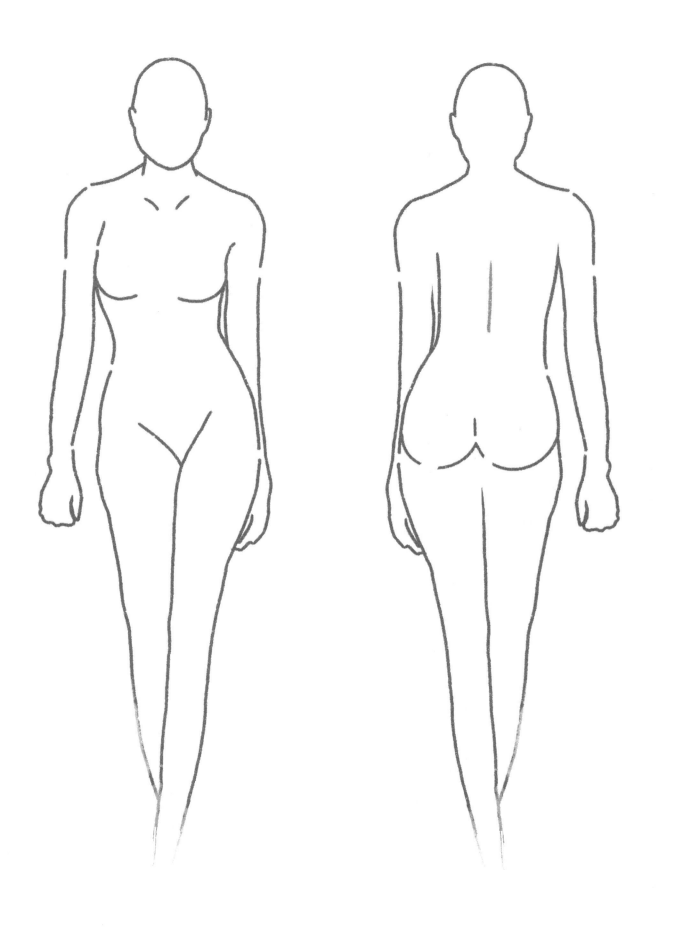

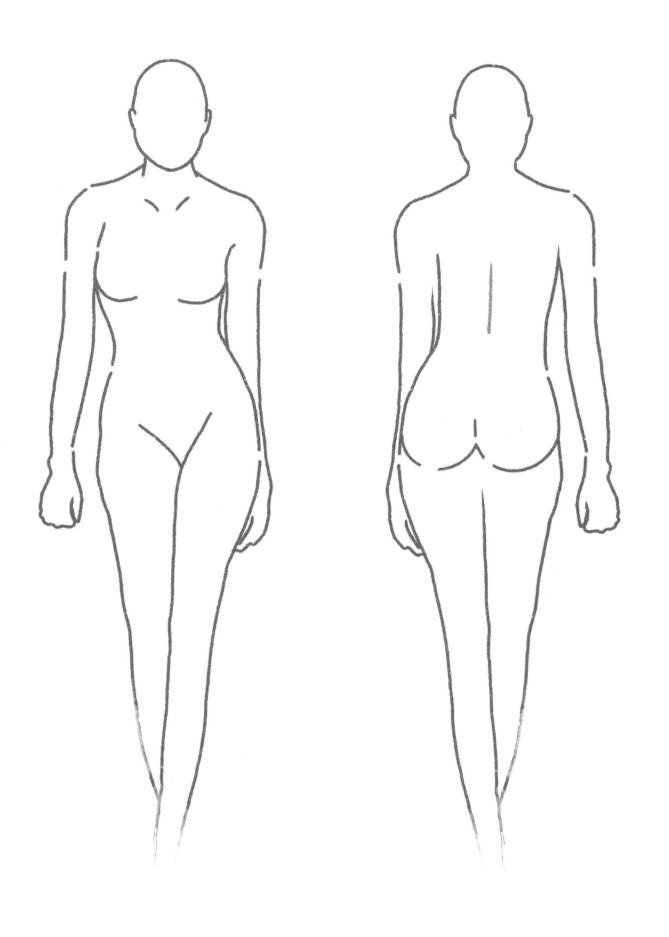

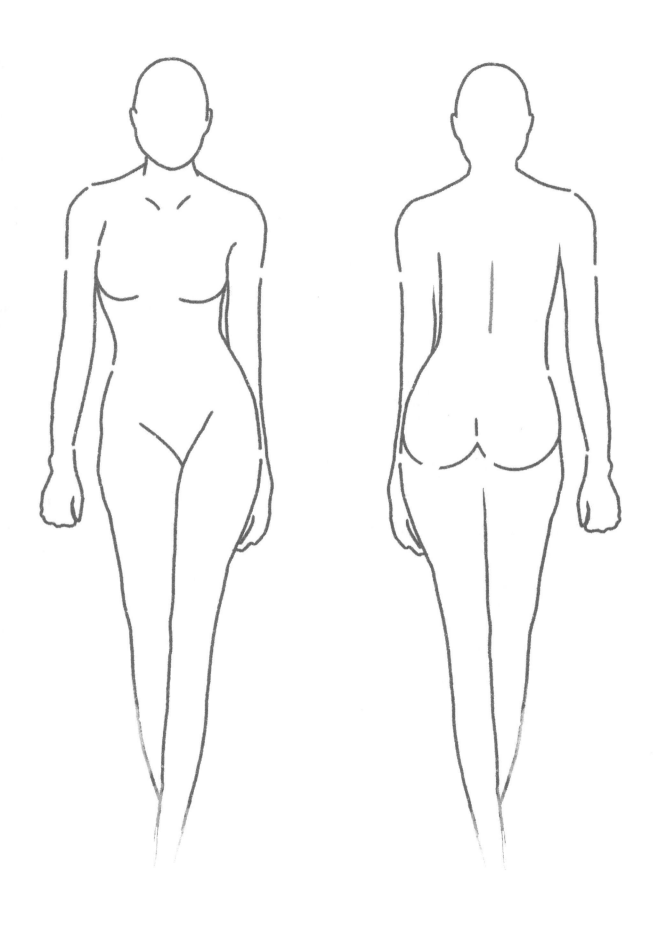

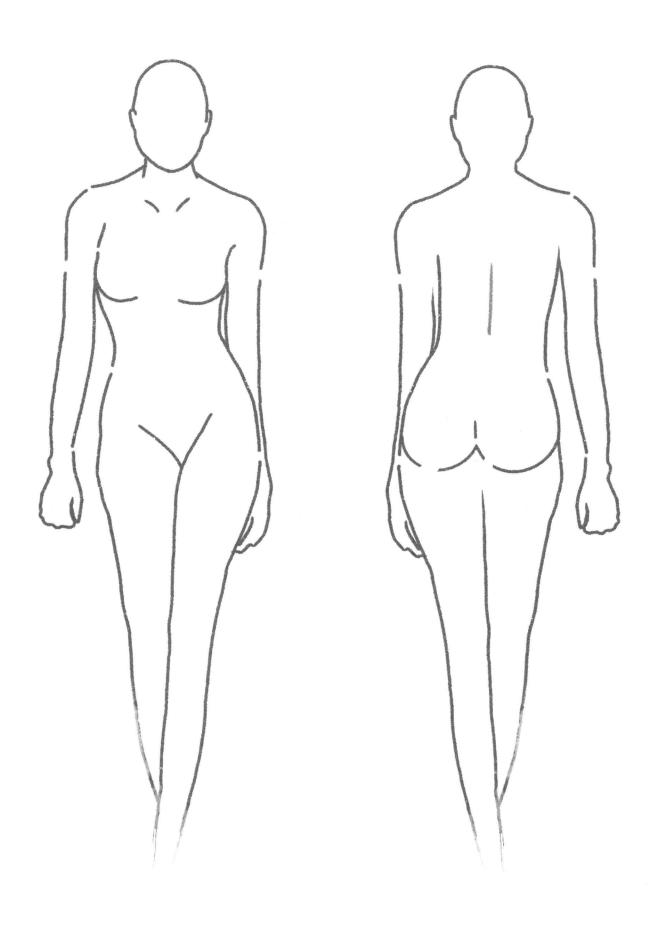

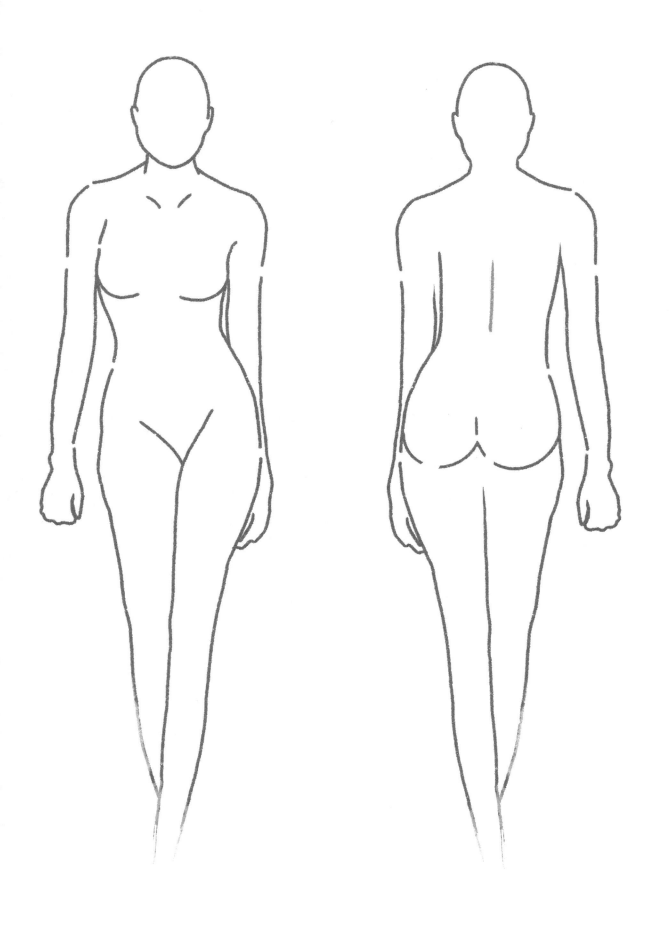

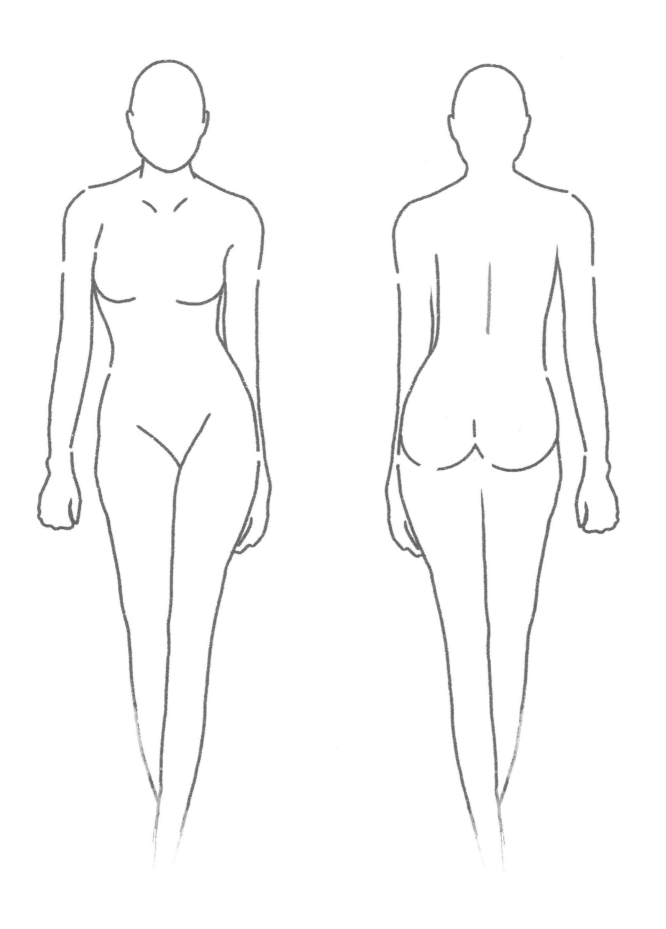

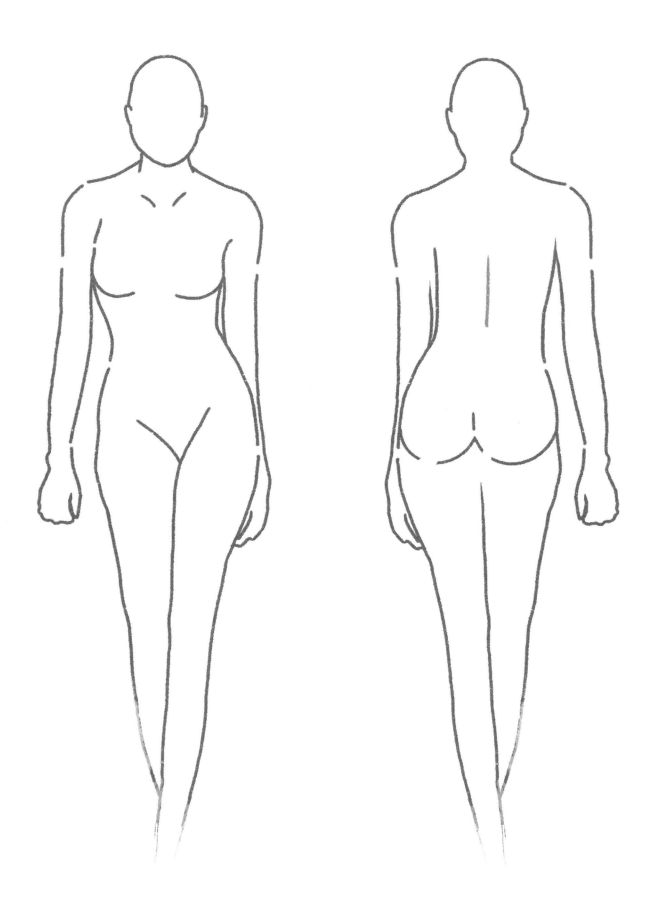

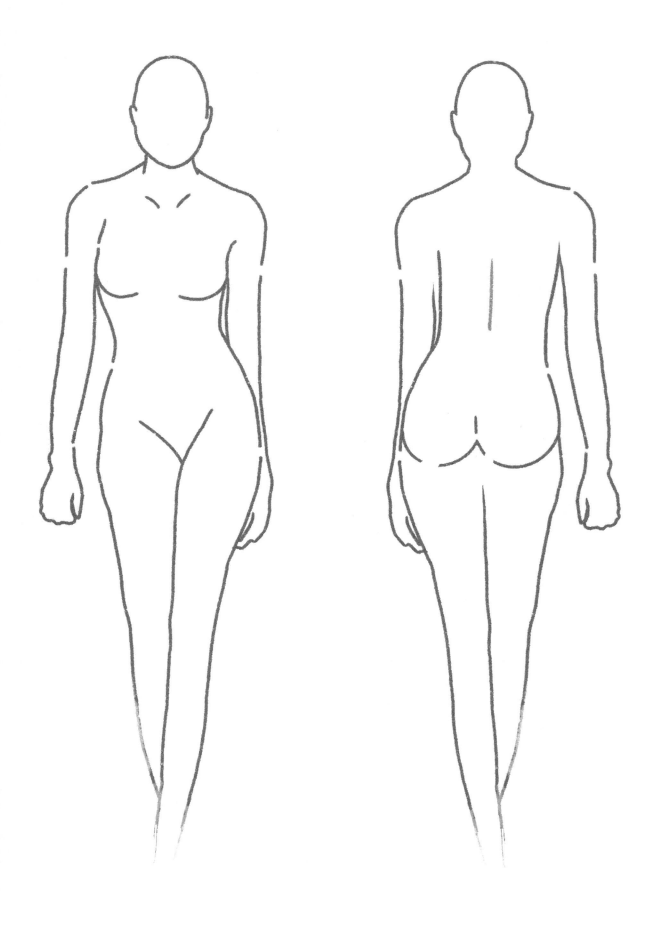

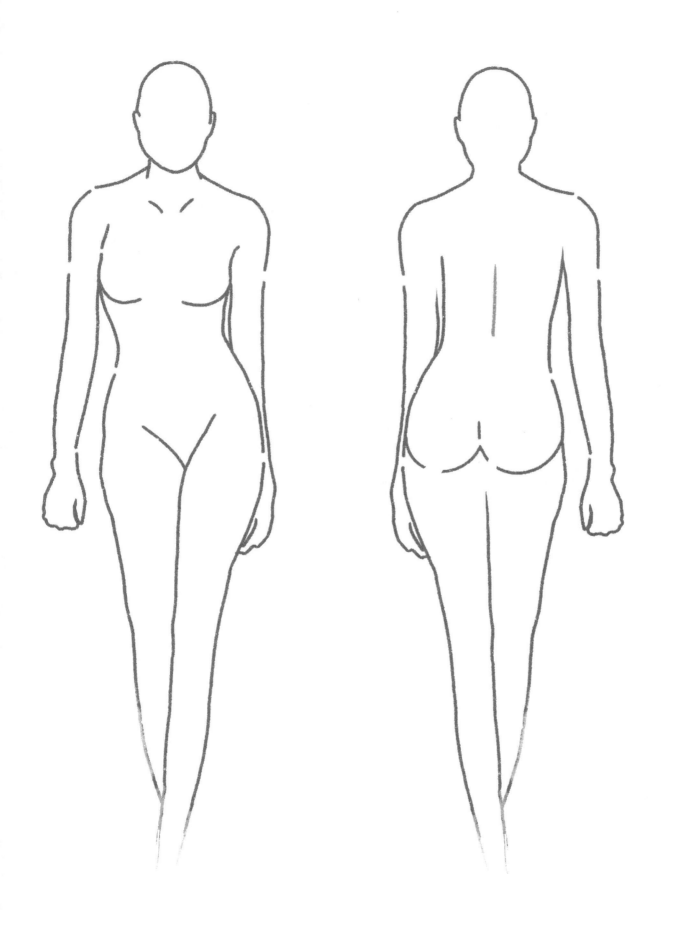

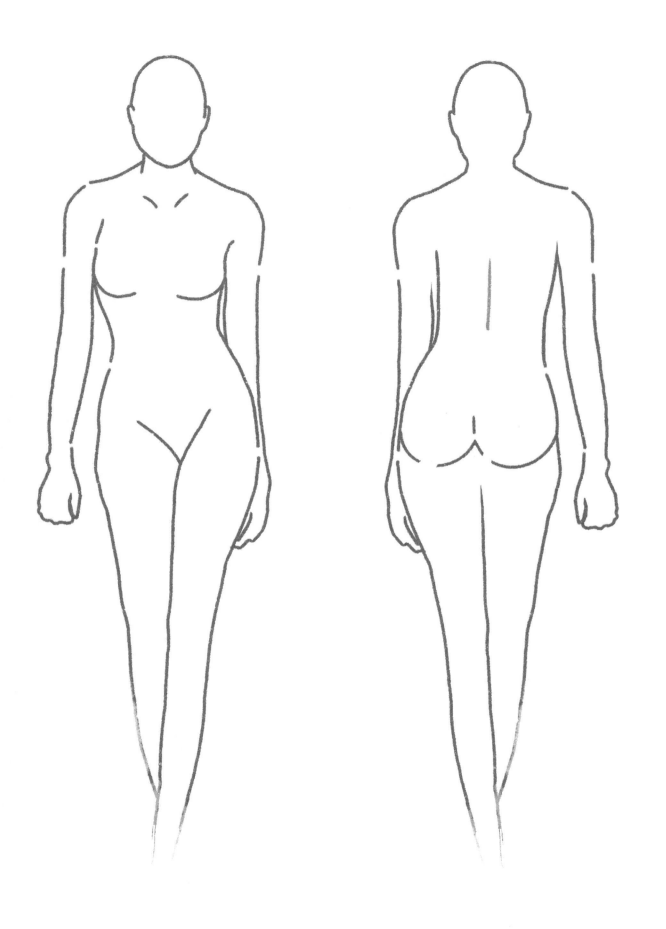

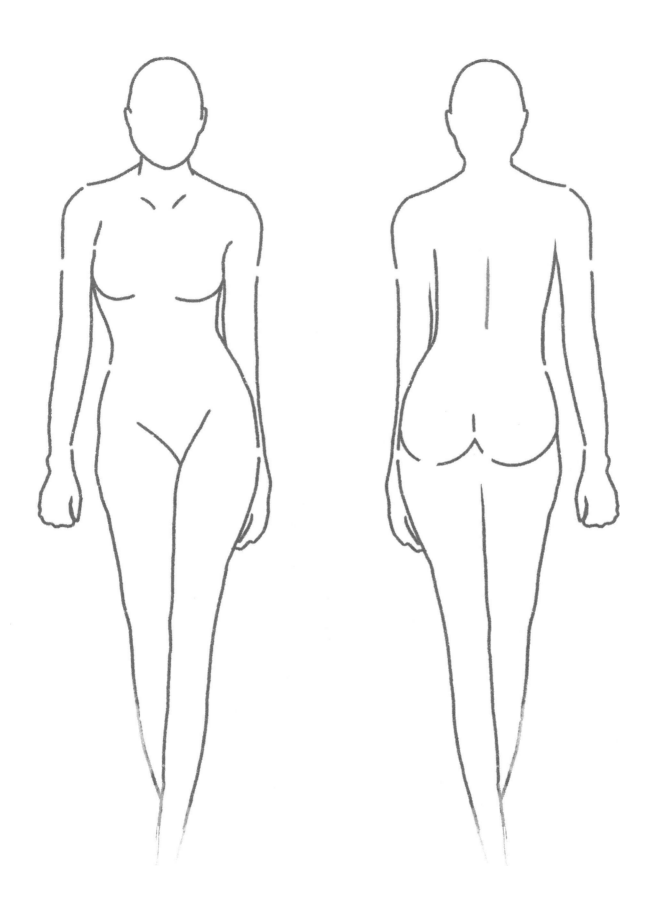

OUTFIT *designer*

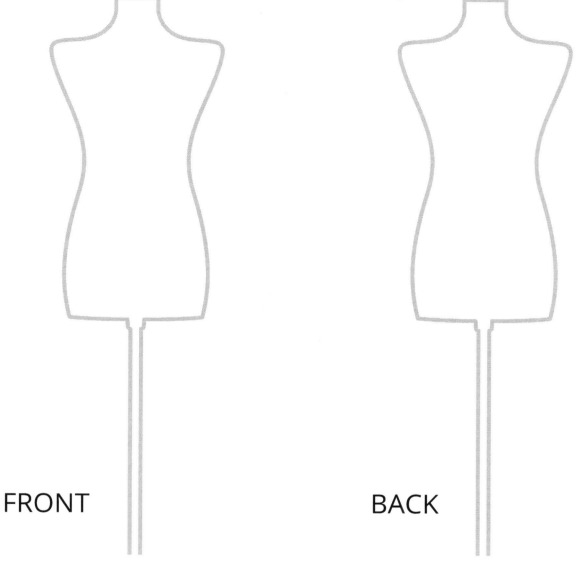

FRONT   BACK

Describe your outfit (what is the occasion/what type
of person would wear it):

OUTFIT *designer*

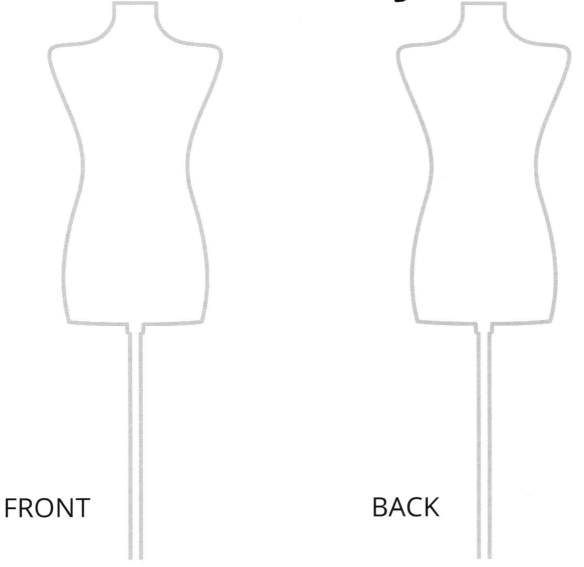

FRONT   BACK

Describe your outfit (what is the occasion/what type
of person would wear it):

OUTFIT
designer

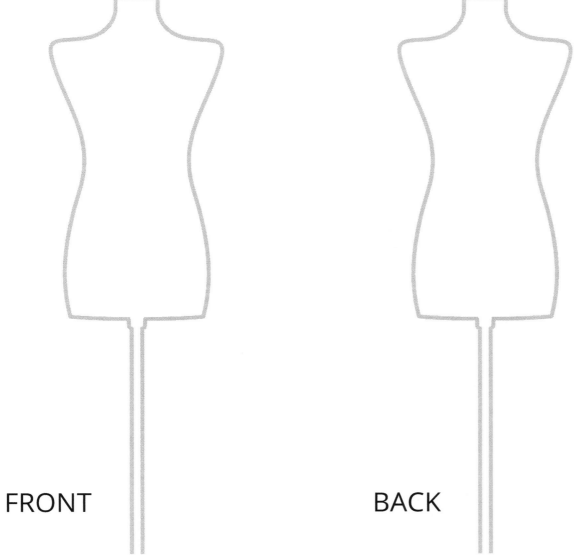

FRONT   BACK

Describe your outfit (what is the occasion/what type of person would wear it):

OUTFIT *designer*

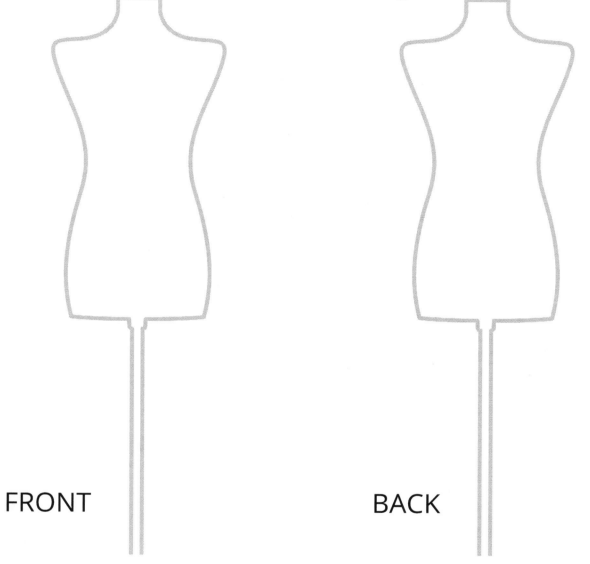

FRONT   BACK

Describe your outfit (what is the occasion/what type of person would wear it):

OUTFIT *designer*

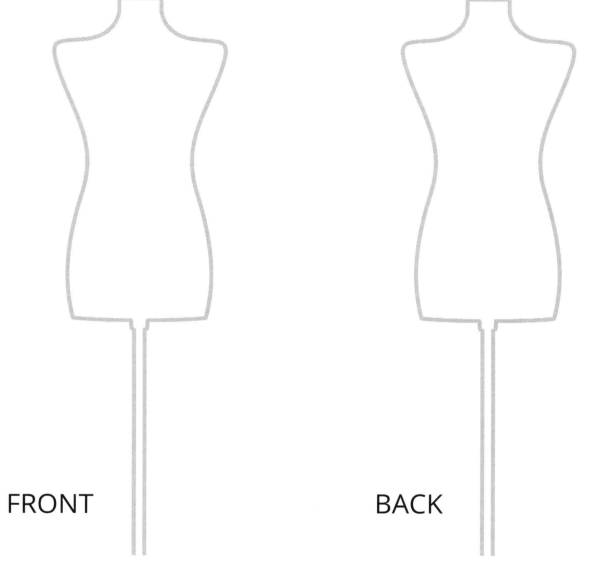

FRONT   BACK

Describe your outfit (what is the occasion/what type of person would wear it):

OUTFIT *designer*

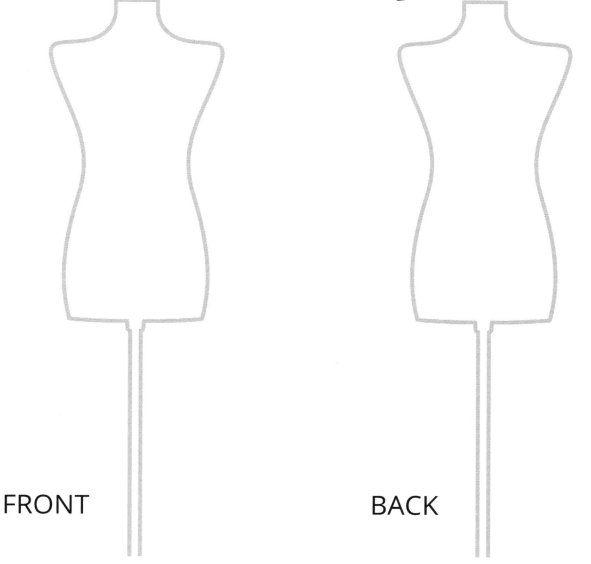

FRONT   BACK

Describe your outfit (what is the occasion/what type of person would wear it):

OUTFIT *designer*

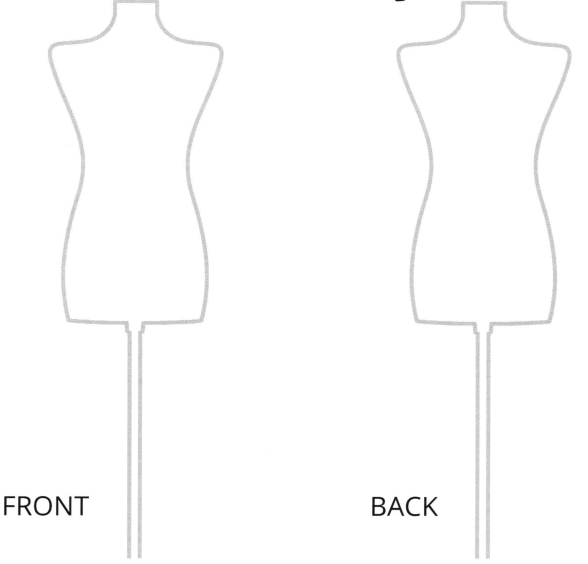

FRONT   BACK

Describe your outfit (what is the occasion/what type of person would wear it):

OUTFIT *designer*

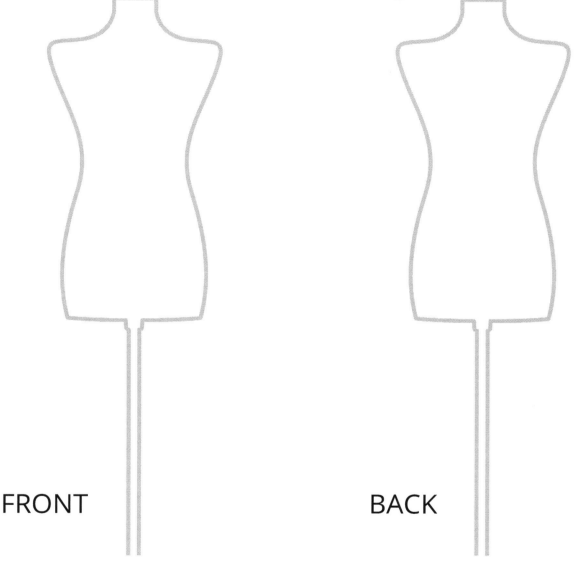

FRONT

BACK

Describe your outfit (what is the occasion/what type of person would wear it):

OUTFIT *designer*

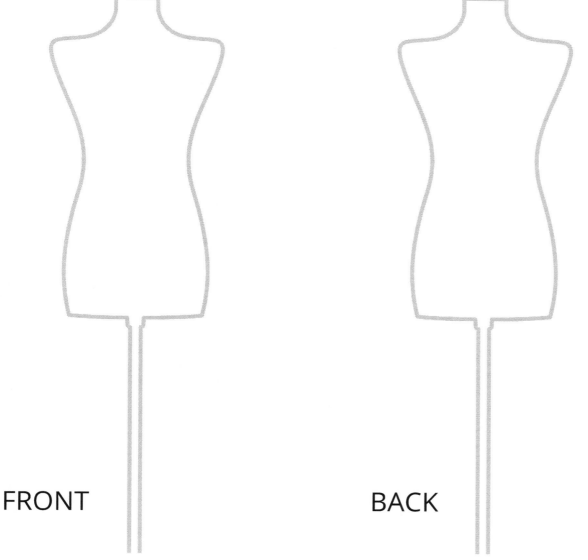

FRONT   BACK

Describe your outfit (what is the occasion/what type of person would wear it):

OTHER AVAILABLE TITLES FROM SAVVY STATIONERY

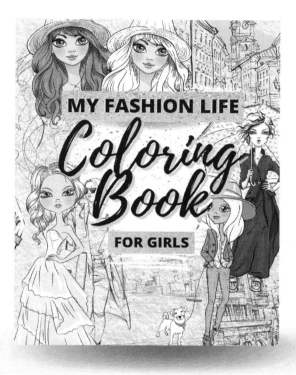

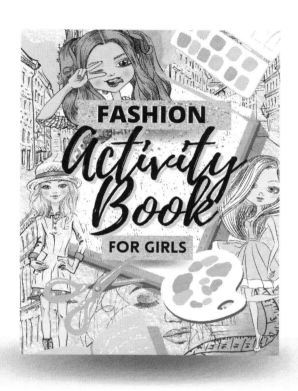

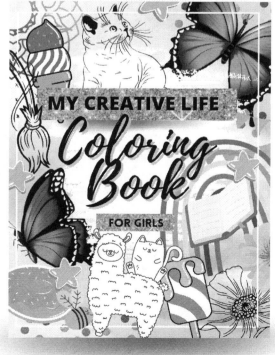

BUY NOW FROM AMAZON!

Made in United States
Troutdale, OR
12/07/2023

15470396R00053